The Science of Living Things
What is a Dog?

Bobbie Kalman & Hannelore Sotzek

Crabtree Publishing Company

The Science of Living Things Series
A Bobbie Kalman Book

Remembering Werner Sotzek
—the leader of the pack

Editor-in-Chief
Bobbie Kalman

Writing Team
Bobbie Kalman
Hannelore Sotzek

Managing Editor
Lynda Hale

Editors
Niki Walker
Heather Levigne
Kate Calder

Copy Editor
Heather Fitzpatrick

Computer Design
Lynda Hale

Production Coordinator
Hannelore Sotzek

Consultant
Dr. Kim Michels,
Doctor of Veterinary Medicine

Special thanks to
Barbara Kolk and the American Kennel Club Library; Karl Baker;
Michael Malaney; Pam Crossley; Nadine, Ceilidh, Suki, and all the
other "models" that appear in this book!

Photographs
Norvia Behling: pages 9, 11 (top), 13, 17, 19 (bottom), 23 (top),
   25, 28 (top), 29 (both)
Marc Crabtree: page 11 (bottom)
Peter Crabtree: page 31
Ron Kimball: front cover, pages 4 (both), 10, 12, 14, 16, 18 (bottom),
   19 (top left and right), 20 (bottom), 21 (top), 26, 27 (top left), 28 (bottom)
Rick Nesbitt: page 3
Reynolds' Stock Photos: pages 20 (top), 21 (bottom), 27 (top right,
   bottom left and right)
Paul Souders/Danita Delimont, Agent: page 22
Stuart Westmorland/Danita Delimont, Agent: page 24
Other images by Digital Stock and Eyewire, Inc.

Illustrations
All illustrations by Barbara Bedell

Digital Prepress
Embassy Graphics

Printer
Worzalla Publishing Company

Crabtree Publishing Company

PMB 16A
350 Fifth Ave.,
Suite 3308
New York, NY
10118

612 Welland Ave.
St. Catharines,
Ontario,
Canada
L2M 5V6

73 Lime Walk
Headington,
Oxford
OX3 7AD
United Kingdom

Cataloging in Publication Data
Kalman, Bobbie
   What is a dog?

(The science of living things)
Includes index.

ISBN 0-86505-979-9 (library bound) ISBN 0-86505-956-X (pbk.)
This book introduces the different kinds of domestic dogs, their behavior,
physiology, uses, diet, and young.

1. Dogs—Juvenile literature. [1. Dogs.] I. Sotzek, Hannelore. II. Title.
III. Series: Kalman, Bobbie. Science of living things.

SF426.5.K36 2000   j636.7   LC 99-085747
                                                        CIP

Contents

What is a dog?

Dogs are **mammals**. Like all mammals, a dog's body is covered with fur or hair. A mammal mother carries her babies inside her body until they are born. After birth, her body makes milk to feed the newborn dogs.

A wolf in dog's clothing

Long ago, all dogs were wild. They lived apart from people and hunted for food. Over time, some wild dogs began living near humans. These wild dogs were wolves. They fed on people's food scraps and were warmed by their fires. Gradually, they became less fearful of people.

(above) Dogs are loyal friends. Many people have pet dogs.

(top) These beagle puppies are feeding on their mother's milk.

Domesticating the wolves

People used some of these wolves for hunting and guarding and, over 10,000 years ago, began **domesticating** them. They trained the dogs to live and work with people. Dogs are some of the first **domestic**, or tame, animals.

People and dogs

After dogs were domesticated, people began **breeding** them to perform specific jobs or have a certain look. They chose dogs with the same traits, such as being able to carry things gently, to **mate** with one another. Their puppies would then also have these traits.

All about breeds

Over the years, mating specific dogs created various **breeds**, or kinds, of dogs. Dogs that are of only one breed are **purebred** animals. Some dogs, however, are a mix of many breeds. These dogs are **mongrels**.

Wild cousins

Today, the dogs that live with people are domestic. Although they came from wolves and may still act wild, dogs do not usually use wild behavior to survive. Most dogs rely on people for their food, whereas their wild cousins hunt for their meals.

The dog family tree

Dogs are members of the **canid** family. There are about 34 **species**, or types, of canids, including wolves, coyotes, jackals, and dingoes. Other types of wild dogs include foxes, dholes, bush dogs, and African wild dogs.

There is only one species of domestic dog, but there are hundreds of breeds. In North America, many of the breeds are commonly divided into seven main groups—sporting dogs, hounds, terriers, working dogs, herding dogs, non-sporting dogs, and toy dogs.

Long, long ago...

Scientists believe that the dog's ancient ancestor was a **carnivorous**, or meat-eating, mammal called the **miacid**. This animal lived millions of years ago. It is also the ancestor of hyenas, cats, raccoons, and bears.

Wolves

The gray wolf and the red wolf are the only true types of wolves. They live mainly in North America, but gray wolves also are found in Asia. The maned wolf, however, is not a wolf at all! This canid lives in South America.

The gray wolf, shown left, is the largest of the wild dogs.

This canid is called the red wolf, but some red wolves have black fur.

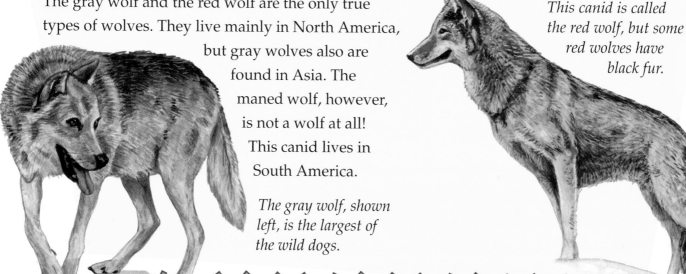

Wild dogs

In the canid family, dogs are grouped with wolves, dingoes, coyotes, and jackals.

Jackals can be found in Asia, Europe, and Africa. The black-backed jackal, shown above, is the only type that lives mainly in Africa.

The dingo of Australia was once a domestic dog but now lives mainly in the wild.

Coyotes make their home in North America.

Domestic dogs

Dog breeds differ greatly in size and shape. The dachshund, for example, has very short legs but a long body. Pugs have a flat face, and the bull terrier has a head that is shaped like a football!

(left) The Irish wolfhound is the tallest breed of dog. It can grow to be three feet (1 m) high.

(right) The smallest breed of dog is the Chihuahua. This dog weighs six pounds (3 kg) or less.

A dog's body

All dogs have a **muzzle**, or snout, a tail, and four legs. A dog's body was originally designed for hunting. Today, most dogs use their muscular body for running and jumping.

A dog uses its tongue for drinking, grooming, and keeping cool. Its sensitive nose is protected by soft padding.

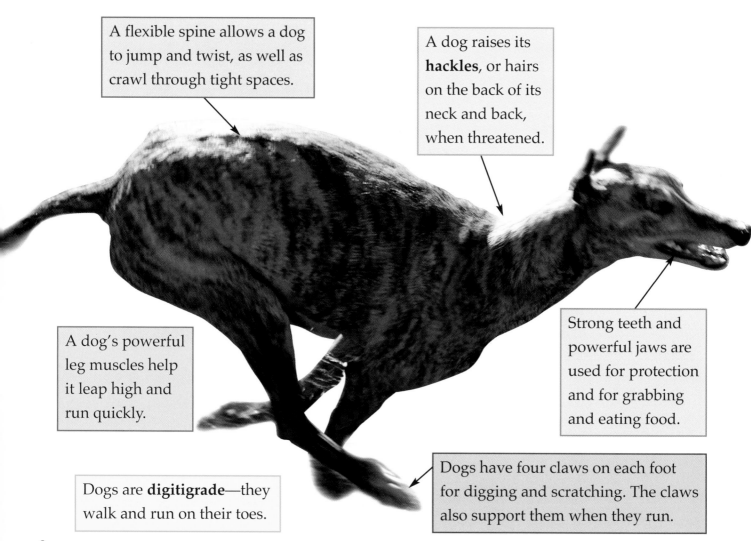

A flexible spine allows a dog to jump and twist, as well as crawl through tight spaces.

A dog raises its **hackles**, or hairs on the back of its neck and back, when threatened.

A dog's powerful leg muscles help it leap high and run quickly.

Strong teeth and powerful jaws are used for protection and for grabbing and eating food.

Dogs are **digitigrade**—they walk and run on their toes.

Dogs have four claws on each foot for digging and scratching. The claws also support them when they run.

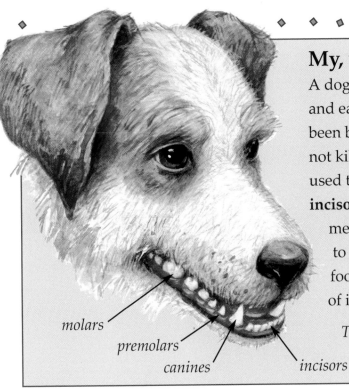

My, what big teeth you have

A dog's teeth were originally designed for killing and eating animals. Many domestic dogs have been bred to have smaller teeth so that they will not kill, but each type of tooth in a dog's jaw is still used to eat meat and other food. A dog uses its **incisors**, or front teeth, to bite things or to scrape meat off bones. It relies on its **canines**, or fangs, to pierce and tear and its **premolars** to hold food. A dog's **molars** are located at the back of its mouth. They are used for chewing food.

The Jack Russell terrier has the same type of teeth as those of a large dog.

molars

premolars

canines

incisors

Many coats

Not all fur coats are the same. The fur of an Afghan hound is silky. The Pekingese has a long-haired coat. Whippets have smooth, short hair. Dogs such as the Irish water spaniel have curly fur, whereas the coat of some terriers is wiry. Retrievers have fur that is suited to being in water, and poodles have coats that do not shed. Komondors have long cords of hair that hang almost to the ground! Other dogs, such as dalmatians, have spotlike markings that identify them.

A few dogs, such as this Chinese crested, have little or no fur at all!

Super senses

Dogs that live in the wild rely on their senses of hearing, smell, and sight to help them hunt and catch other animals, called **prey**, for food. Domestic dogs may also hunt animals, but they use these senses mainly to detect enemies and identify people and objects.

Huh?

Dogs have a great sense of hearing. They can hear a much greater range of sounds than people can. Dogs can hear extremely high-pitched noises. Many small animals such as rats make high-pitched squeaks. By paying attention to these noises, a dog is more likely to find the animals it hunts. A dog's hearing is so keen that a dog can sense the difference between the pattern in the footsteps of someone it knows and those of a stranger.

Many dogs, such as this German shepherd, can raise and turn their large ears in the direction of a sound so they can hear it more clearly.

All the better to smell you...

Dogs have an excellent sense of smell. Their nose is lined with a moist layer called the **nasal epithelium**, which traps scents that a dog **inhales**, or breathes in. Many dogs have a long nose, which gives more room for this lining. Dogs also have a **Jacobson's organ**, which is located in the roof of their mouth. This organ helps dogs detect specific smells and tastes. As a result, dogs can detect a variety of scents. Some scientists believe that a dog's sense of smell is a hundred times greater than that of a human's!

Using its strong sense of smell, a dog can locate the stash of food it has buried.

*Dogs have good nighttime vision. They have a thin layer, called a **tapetum**, in their eyes. This layer reflects light like a mirror to help a dog hunt rodents and other types of prey that are active mainly at night.*

I can see you!

Dogs have good **peripheral vision**—they can see things on either side of their body without having to turn their head. Dogs can see moving objects more quickly than objects that are still. A dog may not notice a motionless squirrel, but it will spot one that is running.

Dogs are **colorblind**, which means they cannot see certain colors. They do not need to see color for hunting. Dogs do see more than black and white, however. Scientists believe that dogs see shades of blue as well as yellow-green. Unlike people, however, dogs cannot see the color red.

Leader of the pack

Dogs usually live in groups called **packs**, which can have two or more members. A dog's pack can be dogs from its family, other dogs, or even people. Dogs are **social** animals—they need the companionship of others. Pack life also provides protection. Dogs warn other members of their pack of dangers, and they protect one another from enemies. Stray dogs may also form a pack to help one another find food because hunting in a group is easier than searching for food alone.

Top dog

Each pack has a **hierarchy**, or order. Every pack member has a place in the hierarchy. The leader is the most **dominant** dog. It is not necessarily the largest dog but the most confident one. All other pack members are **submissive**. These dogs rank below the dominant dog and will not eat before the leader does so first. Having a hierarchy reduces the number of fights in a pack because a submissive dog will not challenge a dominant one.

Beware of dog

A dog's home is its **den**. Dogs mark the boundaries of the pack's **territory**, or the area surrounding their den, with urine and droppings. These marked areas are called **scent posts**. If a dog detects the scent of another animal in its territory, it may cover that scent with its own. In order to defend its territory, a dog will bark at intruders as a warning for them to stay away.

The nose knows

Dogs use smell to identify pack members. **Glands** on their body produce a special scent. A dog can tell whether the dog it is sniffing is dominant or submissive, male or female. Some dogs roll around on an animal carcass or droppings in order to give themselves a stronger odor.

This black dog is showing that it is submissive by dropping to the ground and exposing its belly.

Communication

Dogs **communicate**, or send messages, to other dogs, animals, and people to show others how they are feeling. They use gestures and body language to remind pack members and other animals which place they hold in the pack.

I need attention!

Dogs use touch to give and receive affection. A dog will let you know if it needs attention by tapping or pawing at you. It may even lick you or make noises to get your attention. Touching and licking are also used to spread a dog's scent. Placing its scent on other dogs may help identify them as part of the dog's pack.

Grrrr, woof, yodel-lay-di-hoo

Using sounds is another way dogs communicate. Growling is a threat to enemies, and barking is a warning of danger. When a dog is hurt, it may whine or even yelp. Hounds howl when they are lonely or want to communicate with others, but a basenji does not howl or bark at all. This dog makes a noise that sounds like a yodel!

What do you think this dog is communicating?

When a dog is alert, it raises its ears, showing it is paying attention.

A dog shows it is submissive by hiding its tail between its legs. A tucked tail is harder for an enemy to grab during a fight.

To threaten, a dog stares down its enemy and pulls back its gums to bare its sharp, threatening fangs. If the other animal does not back down, a fight may take place.

To show that it is submissive, a dog may avoid eye contact and hang its head. "Smiling" or pulling back its gums to show all its teeth is another submissive sign.

A raised, quickly wagging tail is a signal of an excited, playful dog.

Puppies

A baby dog is called a puppy. A mother carries her puppies inside her body for about two months before they are born. Just before she is ready to **whelp**, or give birth, the mother finds a warm, sheltered area. There, she gives birth to a **litter**, or group of puppies.

Puppies depend on their mother for food, warmth, and protection. After a puppy is born, its mother licks the puppy's body clean so it can breathe and urinate. A mother **grooms**, or cleans, her puppies until they can groom themselves.

A female dog can have up to two litters per year. The size of a litter varies with the breed. Depending on the type of dog, a litter may have only one puppy or as many as eighteen puppies!

Puppy chow

Right after a puppy is born, it searches for food. The puppy pulls itself toward its mother and drinks milk from her teats. At three weeks, its teeth begin to show and the puppy is ready to be **weaned**. It stops drinking its mother's milk and starts eating soft food, which is easy for a puppy's body to **digest**, or break down. Mothers can even **regurgitate**, or spit up, food for their babies. By about six weeks of age, most puppies are able to eat solid food.

Growing up

During the first two weeks of its life, a puppy mainly eats and sleeps. It cannot hear or see. Eventually, its eyes open. Its ears also open so the puppy can hear. At four to six weeks of age, the young dog is ready to begin exploring. At twelve weeks, it is more active and curious but still is not able to live without care and protection.

Playing tug-of-war helps develop a puppy's hunting skills. Tugging represents an action similar to that of pulling apart prey.

Sporting dogs

Long ago, people bred sporting dogs, also known as **gun dogs**, to help hunt birds. There are four main types of sporting dogs—retrievers, pointers, setters, and spaniels. They all have excellent tracking and hunting skills.

Retrievers

Retrievers were bred to find and retrieve prey, especially in water. Their thick, oily coat helps keep water off their skin. Most retrievers are excellent swimmers and will swim long distances to fetch water birds such as ducks. Chesapeake Bay retrievers have **webbed** feet. The membranes connecting their toes help them swim better.

Retrievers carry an animal gently so that their teeth will not pierce the prey.

Pointers and setters

Pointers and setters find prey and show hunters where it is located. When these dogs detect a bird, they do not chase it. A pointer stands still and "points" with its body to the resting spot of the prey. Setters do not point. Instead, they drop to the ground and direct hunters toward the prey.

(above left) A pointer holds its position until it is told to move.
(above) An English setter's heavy fur coat protects its body from brush and rough grasses.

Spaniels

Spaniels were first bred to **flush** out, or startle, animals resting in the grass and bushes. These dogs are shorter than other types of sporting dogs. Their body is close to the ground, which allows them to sneak up on prey hiding in long grasses.

(right) The cocker spaniel is the smallest type of sporting dog. It can run quickly for long periods of time.

Hounds

Originally, hounds were bred to hunt forest animals such as rabbits, foxes, deer, bears, and elk. There are two categories of hounds—sight and scent hounds.

Sight hounds

Sight hounds have good eyesight and can spot their prey easily. With sudden bursts of speed, these long-legged dogs run swiftly to chase a quick meal such as a rabbit.

Scent hounds

Scent hounds use their keen sense of smell to track animals. Many hounds have a body that is close to the ground, allowing them to sniff out animals that live underground, such as foxes and badgers. Hounds can chase their prey for a long time. When the prey tires out, it is easier to catch.

(above) The Afghan hound's long silky coat developed as a way of keeping this dog warm in its mountain home in Afghanistan.

Many types of scent hounds, such as this basset hound, have long ears that they cannot raise fully. Some people believe that drooping ears help hounds pick up scents on the ground.

Terriers

Terriers were bred to hunt small animals such as rats, which make their home in the ground. Some terriers help hunters by chasing prey out of their burrows. Others kill the prey themselves. There are two groups of terriers—short-legged and long-legged terriers.

Short-legged terriers

Short-legged terriers have a small body that is suited to working in narrow or underground spaces. These dogs use their front feet to dig into a prey's burrow. When digging in tunnels, short-legged terriers kick rocks and dirt aside so they will not bury themselves under the loose dirt.

Long-legged terriers

Long-legged terriers are too big to hunt in burrows. Instead, they dig up the earth with their long, narrow legs and kick the unwanted dirt behind them. Many long-legged terriers have floppy ears, which prevent the dirt from getting inside them.

The Cairn terrier became popular in Scotland where it chased prey such as foxes, which live in rocky areas. The word "cairn" refers to a pile of stones.

The Staffordshire bull terrier differs from most other long-legged terriers. It has a broad chest and widely placed legs and was originally bred for fighting.

Working dogs

Most working dogs have a large, muscular body, which makes them well suited for guarding, rescuing, and **hauling**, or pulling. They learn quickly and perform jobs well. Great Danes, Newfoundlands, rottweilers, and boxers are examples of working dogs.

Sled dog racing is a challenging sport. The Iditarod Trail Sled Dog Race in Alaska covers a distance of 1,150 miles (1850 km) and can take ten to seventeen days to complete. In a long-distance race such as this, one sled dog team uses between twelve and sixteen huskies.

Hauling dogs

Many working dogs are trained to haul loads. Some pull carts filled with crops or heavy items. Teams of dogs are often used to pull sleds of people and supplies over ice and snow.

Guard dogs

Guard dogs are strong, alert, and look threatening. Police rely on them to perform risky tasks in dangerous situations. Many people use guard dogs to protect themselves and their property.

Rescue dogs

Rescue dogs work in emergency situations. They assist people who are in danger. Some search mountainsides for victims of avalanches. Others are powerful swimmers that assist rescue efforts at sea.

Doberman pinschers make good watchdogs because they are obedient and quick.

Saint Bernards can find travelers lost in snow. They help revive victims by licking their face. These dogs also keep people warm by lying next to them. The warmth of their large body helps keep the victims alive.

Herding dogs

Herding dogs help farmers look after **livestock** such as sheep and cattle. They gather the animals and guide them from one place to another to make sure they do not get lost. They also help protect livestock from **predators**, or animals that hunt and eat other animals for food. All dogs may hunt, but herding dogs are trained not to hunt the animals they are protecting.

Many herding dogs have coats that help them blend in with their surroundings. Old English sheepdogs have long gray fur that is similar to a sheep's wool. This type of **camouflage** helps the dogs hide among the animals they are protecting. The dogs can then startle unsuspecting enemies. Their thick coat also protects their body during fights with predators and other enemies.

The border collie is originally from Scotland but is now used for herding on farms all over the world. This collie is rounding up a herd of piglets.

Herding styles

Each dog has its own method of herding livestock. Some chase after sheep that stray from the flock and direct them back to the group. Others run around the entire group of livestock to gather and herd them in the proper direction. On some farms, herding dogs work alone, and on others, the dogs work in groups.

Welsh corgis have short legs, so their body is low to the ground. These small dogs are not scared by the larger animals they guard. To direct sheep or cattle that have strayed, the Welsh corgi nips at their heels.

non-sporting dogs

Originally, there were two main dog groups—sporting and non-sporting. Today, there are seven groups. Many breeds that were not bred to be sporting dogs now belong to the non-sporting group. The dogs in this group vary greatly in their body types and abilities.

Years ago, dalmatians ran beside a horse and carriage to protect its passengers from robbers. Later, dalmatians were used by firefighters. The dogs kept control of the horses that pulled the fire-fighting wagons.

(above) Keeshonds were popular dogs in Holland, where they were used as guard dogs on farms and boats.

(above) The chow chow is among the oldest breeds of dogs, existing for more than 2,000 years! Today, it is well known for its blue-black tongue.

(below) The Lhasa apso was kept as a guard dog in Tibetan holy places.

(above) The Chinese Shar-pei is known for its short, rough coat and wrinkled skin. Its name means "sand skin." It is one of two dog breeds that has a blue-black tongue.

Toy dogs

Toy dogs are the smallest dog breeds. They have been bred from larger dogs including hounds, sporting dogs, and terriers. Toy dogs provide company and protection for people.

A perfect fit

Toy dogs are often called **lap dogs** because they fit comfortably on a person's lap. A toy dog can be picked up and carried easily. Its small size makes it ideal for living in small places such as apartments. Toy dogs do not need much room for exercise and are well suited to living in cities.

Protective pals

Although toy dogs may not seem fierce or threatening, many can be aggressive when they need to be. Toys are extremely protective of their territory and pack. Their sharp bark is a warning to strangers to stay out of their territory.

(top) The Shih Tzu's name comes from a Chinese word meaning "lion."

(left) The Chihuahua is named after a state in Mexico.

Dogs in danger

Since people have taken dogs from the wild, they are responsible for them. If people do not take proper care of their dogs, the animals can suffer from sickness, abuse, and other dangers.

Puppy mills

A **puppy mill**, shown right, is a business owned by a person who breeds many dogs to make as much money as possible. Female dogs are kept to produce puppies. Having so many litters causes a dog to become sick and die. The puppies that are born are often unhealthy as well.

The problem with breeding

Different breeds have developed because people have created their idea of the ideal dog. Some breeds have disappeared because people no longer breed them. The white English terrier is an **extinct** breed—no more of these dogs exist. Breeding has also created health problems in some dogs. Bulldogs and boxers have been bred not to have the long muzzle that other dogs have. The short muzzle causes them to have difficulties in breathing.

A bulldog pup's head is often too big for the mother's body to birth naturally, or without the help of people. This bulldog's lower jaw is out so far that it cannot chew its food easily.

Our best friends

For many people, a dog is not just a playmate and protector but a best friend. Having a dog is fun, but it is also work. Dogs need food, water, shelter, exercise, and a lot of attention to become happy, healthy pets. Do you have a dog?

Bathing a dog can be a wet experience! These girls are ready for a soaking.

The best home for Fido

There are many breeds and types of dogs from which to choose. It is important to choose a dog that is right for you. You need to find out if your dog will live indoors or outside, how much exercise it needs, and what it will cost to feed it.

Where to find a dog

Some people buy a dog from a store. Others get their puppy from a friend. Dogs can also be adopted from animal shelters or organizations that rescue abused, abandoned, or lost dogs.

Run, Fido, run

Dogs need a lot of exercise. They are built to run and be active. Many dogs become restless if they are left alone for long periods of time. They may find other ways to release their energy, such as chewing furniture or hiding shoes. Taking a dog for a walk and having it run and fetch sticks or balls are good ways to exercise your dog.

Feeding and grooming

Dogs need to eat the proper amount of dog food for their age and weight. Table scraps can have too much fat and salt and be unhealthy for dogs. Dogs often groom themselves, but they also need baths to remove dirt from their fur or hair. Ask your **veterinarian**, or animal doctor, to tell you the best way to feed and care for your breed of dog.

No bad dogs!

Proper obedience training teaches people how to handle their dog so that it will not hurt others or be hurt itself. Dogs learn to respond to commands such as "sit," "stay," and "come." Obedience training also helps a dog get used to strangers and other dogs. The dog learns not to be shy or afraid of others.

*Regular visits to a veterinarian help keep a dog healthy. A veterinarian **vaccinates** animals to prevent them from contracting rabies and other serious diseases. "Say aah!"*

Words to know

ancestor An early animal from which later species developed

breed (n) A group of animals in a species having similar traits; (v) to cause two selected animals to mate

burrow An animal's underground home or hiding spot

camouflage Colors or markings on an animal that hide it in natural surroundings

domesticate To tame and train an animal to live with people and be useful to them

dominant Describing someone or something that has the most control

gland A sac inside the body that produces and releases a substance such as liquid

mate To join together to make babies

mongrel A dog that has an unknown background or has come from many breeds

purebred Describing a dog that has parents that are the same breed

species A group of similar living things that can make babies with one another

stray dogs Lost or abandoned dogs

submissive Describing a living being that will let another being control it

track To follow a trail such as the scent of an animal

vaccinate To inject a person or animal with a vaccine that helps protect against specific diseases

Index

1 2 3 4 5 6 7 8 9 0 Printed in the U.S.A. 9 8 7 6 5 4 3 2 1 0